The De
of Arbroath

What it meant then
and what it means now

TOM TURPIE

Luath Press Limited
EDINBURGH
www.luath.co.uk

DR TOM TURPIE is a lecturer in History at the University of Stirling. Originally from New Eltham in South London, Tom completed his doctorate at the University of Edinburgh in 2011 on the subject of the cult of the saints in Medieval Scotland. He is the author of several articles on that subject and a 2015 book entitled *Kind Neighbours: Scottish Saints and Society in the Later Middle Ages* (Brill Publishers, Leiden). Since completing his doctorate, Tom has taught medieval history at Edinburgh and Stirling, and has collaborated on a number of academic and community history projects, including the Family Names UK Project (2013–4), the Fife Pilgrim Way (2016), Kilrenny, Anstruther and Cellardyke Burgh Survey (2016–7) and Inverkeithing Community Burgh Survey (2019–).

First published 2020
Reprinted 2022, 2023

ISBN: 978-1-913025-67-0

The paper used in this book is recyclable.
It is made from low chlorine pulps
produced in a low energy, low emissions
manner from renewable forests.

Printed and bound by
Robertson Printers, Forfar

Typeset in Quadraat
by 3btype.com

The author's right to be identified as author
of this work under the Copyright, Designs
and Patents Act 1988 has been asserted.

Contents

Preface

I first encountered The Declaration of Arbroath as a boy, reading Nigel Tranter's epic *Bruce Trilogy* on holiday. In Tranter's masterly but sympathetic take on the career of Robert I of Scotland, the letter is a statement of a nation, signed by hundreds and reflecting the widespread support for the hero king. When I next encountered it, as an undergraduate student, I was intrigued to find that scholarly research has shown that it is a far more complex and interesting document than the one found in Tranter's account. Historians have focused on the way it was put together, the immediate diplomatic and political context in which it was produced, and traced its reception down the centuries. As a researcher, my main focus has been on the section that explores the origins and history of the kingdom of the Scots, and the development of their relationship with St Andrew. It was finally as a university teacher, exploring the significance of this document with students native to Scotland and from across the globe, that the longer-term influence that this letter has had on Scotland and beyond became clear. What has also become clear from this experience is that understanding of the purpose and content of the letter produced in 1320 beyond university academics is limited. This book will attempt to address this, answering readers' questions of why and how the Declaration was produced, why it includes the sentiments it does, allowing you to appreciate and enjoy this vital and relevant piece of Scotland's past as I do.

Note on terminology

The Declaration was originally one of three letters delivered to the Pope by Scottish envoys in the summer of 1320 and only became known as the Declaration of Arbroath fairly recently. It is referred to in this book as 'the Barons' Letter' or 'the letter'. All translations from the original Latin of the text into English used in the book, as well as the Latin text itself, follow Sir James Fergusson, *The Declaration of Arbroath, 1320* (Edinburgh, 1970).

Timeline

1305	William Wallace captured and executed
1306 (February)	Robert Bruce murders John Comyn at Dumfries Greyfriars Kirk for which he is automatically excommunicated, inaugurated at Scone as Robert I on 25 March
1307 (July)	Death of Edward I, succeeded by Edward II
1308–10	Robert I personally absolved by Pope for murder of Comyn
1309	Declarations of the Scottish Clergy and Nobility sent to Philip IV, justifying support for Robert I
1314 (June)	Scottish victory at the Battle of Bannockburn
1315–22	Great European Famine
1315	Robert I excommunicated for invasion of Ireland
1317	'Remonstrance of the Irish Princes' – letter sent to Pope John XXII from Ireland with similar theme to Declaration of Arbroath
1317	Truce between Scots and English forces declared by Pope John XXII
1318 (October)	Death of Edward Bruce at the Battle of Faughert in Ireland
1319	Bovine Pestilence
1319	Robert I excommunicated by Pope John XXII and Papal Bulls summon the King and four bishops to Avignon for 1 May 1320
1320 (March)	Meeting of General Council at Newbattle
(April)	Declaration of Arbroath sent to Pope John XXII at his palace in Avignon

(August)	Pope John XXII suspends excommunication of Robert I and four Scottish bishops
1327 (January)	Edward II deposed and murdered by English opposition and is succeeded by Edward III
1328 (March)	Treaty of Edinburgh-Northampton ends First War of Independence
1329 (June)	Death of Robert I, succeeded by David II
1332	Edward Balliol invades Scotland and starts Second War of Independence, David II forced into exile
1337	Beginning of Hundred Years' War limits English support for Balliol
1341	David II returns from exile
1346	David II captured at the Battle of Neville's Cross
1356	Balliol gives up claim to Scottish throne
1357	David II ransomed and Second War ends
1689	First publication of the Barons' Letter by itself and in translation from Latin to English
1776	United States Declaration of Independence
1904	A local historian, J Brodie, first used the term Declaration of Arbroath
1998	Senate Resolution 155 officially designated 6 April, the date on the Declaration of Arbroath, as Tartan Day in the US
2016	Declaration of Arbroath placed on UNESCO's Memory of the World register

Reproduction of the 'Tyninghame' (1320AD) copy of the Declaration of Arbroath

Introduction

Non enim propter gloriam,
diuicias aut honores pugnamus set propter
libertatem solummodo quam Nemo bonus nisi
simul cum vita amittit.

It is in truth not for glory, nor riches,
nor honours that we are fighting,
but for freedom — for that alone which no
honest man gives up but with life itself

These words are from a letter or petition that has been known since the early 20th century as the Declaration of Arbroath. It was written in the name of the barons, freeholders and community of the kingdom of Scotland and sent in April 1320 to Pope John XXII at his palace in Avignon.

After 700 years the words retain their power as a clarion call for resistance against tyranny. Found on the walls of classrooms and public houses across Scotland and beyond, it is one of the most celebrated and quoted, but least understood, of the relics from the nation's past. For modern day Scots interested in that past, or in their country's political future, it is generally identified as an influential document, and sometimes as a vital early statement of national identity. More recently, when, in 1998, the United States Senate officially designated 6 April as Tartan Day, the resolution also made mention of the 'Scottish Declaration of Independence' and formally recorded that their own Declaration of Independence was 'modelled on that inspirational document'. For historians who have given the document their serious attention since the 1960s, things are less clear cut. The production, content, impact and significance of the letter all remain areas of controversy and debate.

On the 700th anniversary of this document, this book uses up-to-date academic research to explain why the letter was produced and why it contains the extraordinary sentiments it does. It sets it in the context of a world plagued by war, dynastic disputes and climate change, and explores how the relevance of this letter has ebbed and flowed over seven centuries. In doing so, the aim is to help readers understand the single most celebrated document to be produced in medieval Scotland.

SECTION I

Scotland, England and the Papacy in the Middle Ages

Medieval Scotland

*in exili degentes Scocia vltra quam
habitacio non est*

*poor little Scotland, beyond which
there is no dwelling-place at all*

To understand the Barons' Letter, and particularly its style and content, it is important to understand the nature of the kingdom that produced it, and the political and environmental situation in the years leading up to 1320. The kingdom of the Scots was a small state located on the peripheries of Europe, with a population of between 500,000 and one million. Despite their location, the Scots were not an isolated community. They were bound to the rest of the British Isles, Scandinavia and Continental Europe by strong political, commercial and cultural ties. The sophisticated arguments made within the Barons' Letter testify to this. Scotland was a monarchical state with supreme power in the hands of kings, who from the 1050s had belonged to what we now call the Canmore dynasty. This royal house had, over several centuries, been aggressively expansionist, extending their rule west and north from a base in east, central and southern Scotland. Following a victory over the Norwegians at the Battle of Largs in 1263 and the subsequent Treaty of Perth (1266), the area whose inhabitants gave homage to the King of Scots (in name at least) covered all of what is now modern Scotland, apart from the northern Isles of Orkney and Shetland (annexed to the kingdom in 1470).

Aside from the King, political power was in the hands of a small group of men and women who inherited or were granted titles and land, known as the nobles or aristocracy. The top-ranking nobility were the earls, men who had considerable local autonomy in regions under their control, and below them were the barons, major land-owners in their own right. Since the 1070s, the native Gaelic speak-ing nobility had been joined by large numbers of men from Normandy, Brittany and Flanders. Often arriving via England, where the Scottish kings held lands, this new Anglo-Norman aristocracy had arrived at the invitation of these monarchs who had settled them in both the heartlands and frontier regions of the kingdom. They played a major role in helping the Canmore dynasty to extend their power as they brought with them the cutting-edge military technology of castle construction and the mounted knight, which had proved so decisive in the Norman conquest of England. They helped the Canmores to defeat a series of rival claimants to the throne and maintain a relatively equal relationship with the powerful neighbour-ing kingdom of England. They also brought with them a new method of land ownership, known as the Feudal system, by which the nobles were granted land by the King in return for military and other services. Through the encouragement of the crown and inter-marriage with these new families, the native nobles of Scotland were slowly integrated into this new system of relationships, and into the cultural world of western Europe.

At the same time as this political transformation, the kingdom underwent significant economic and religious changes. The Scottish kings founded small market centres called burghs in places like Berwick, Edinburgh, Stirling, Dundee and Aberdeen, to act as hubs for international trade. They were populated, initially at least, by men from England, Flanders and northern France, who brought with them international contacts and skills in crafts like metal working. They also brought new languages, most notably a form of northern English that would eventually become known as 'Scots', which would then force Gaelic into a long retreat north and west. The religious landscape was also transformed with the introduction in the 12th century of a European-style church structure, made up of Bishops, dioceses and parishes, replacing the older Celtic and Saxon forms of Christianity previously practised in the kingdom. In the 1190s, the independence of this Scottish Church was formally recognised by the Popes, the leaders of the Western Christian Church, who granted it the status of 'Special Daughter of the See of Rome'. This meant that the Scottish Bishops were able to run the church themselves, with the Pope as nominal overlord, free of interference from England. The Scottish kings also invited new European monastic orders to Scotland in the 12th century – orders such as the Augustinians and Cistercians, and in the 13th century, the Franciscans and Dominicans. They built fine new abbey churches, such as the one at which the Declaration was produced, a house of monks of the order of Tiron, founded at Arbroath by King William I in 1178.

Recent scholarship has shown that around the same time that the independence of the Scottish Church was secured in the late 12th century, Scotland's political and intellectual elite began to develop a new and clear sense of Scottishness. This identity was not based on language or ethnicity, as with modern nationalism that developed in the 18th and 19th centuries. This would not have made sense in the polyglot and multi-ethnic 13th century kingdom. It was based on a shared past and, most importantly, an obedience to the King of Scots. This identity was articulated in a chronicle, probably written by a man called Richard Vairemont in the 1260s, which was the first large-scale attempt at a history of the kingdom.

This history emphasised the long pedigree of the Kings and of their connection to an equally long-established Church, provided with a patron saint by the miraculous arrival of the relics of the apostle St Andrew in Fife in the 4th century AD. These arguments for the sovereignty of the kingdom would play an important part in the Declaration of Arbroath.

This process of political, economic and religious change meant that, by 1286, all modern Scotland (except the northern Isles) had been gradually transformed from a Celtic kingdom into a coherent, European-style state with a clear sense of identity that would be strongly expressed in the Declaration of Arbroath. The existence of this identity, and the institutions (Church, Crown, Law) that supported it, were some of the key reasons that successive English kings found it so difficult, and ultimately impossible, to conquer Scotland after war broke out in 1296.

Things Fall Apart:
War and Climate Change,
c.1250–1320

Ita quippe quod gens nostra sub ipsorum proteccione
hactenus libera deguit et quieta

our nation under their protection did indeed
live in freedom and peace

[in 1266] very great storm arose from the north, as a result of which
the sea, whipped up into a frenzy and overstepping its proper limits
in an extraordinary way, flattened houses, farms and trees,
and caused a great deal of damage in many places, but especially
between the rivers of Tay and Tweed.[1]

Scotichronicon, WALTER BOWER, 1440s

The 'freedom and peace' of the 13th-century kingdom of the Scots came to an end as a result of a combined ecological and political crisis. From the mid-13th century, there was a change across northern Europe to a colder, wetter and more unpredictable climate, as the storms of the year 1266 demonstrated. The previously benign climate period known as the Medieval Warm Period (c.950–1250) was replaced by what we now know as the Little Ice Age (c.1250–1750), a period of unsettled climatic conditions

---

1   Watt, Donald ER, ed. *Scotichronicon by Walter Bower in Latin and English* (Aberdeen: University Press, 1987–99), v, pp. 359-61.

(particularly intense in the period c.1250–1350). These new conditions caused considerable problems for medieval agriculture and disrupted trade and transport routes. These environmental problems coincided with a political crisis in Scotland, brought on by the failure of the Canmore dynasty. On 19 March 1286, Alexander III, who had occupied the throne since 1249, died in a tragic accident. On a stormy March evening, Alexander was on his way to visit his new French queen, Yolande of Dreux, when he became separated from his guards only to be found the next morning on the beach at Kinghorn in Fife with a broken neck. Alexander's first queen (Margaret, sister of Edward I of England) had died in 1275 and their three children, Margaret (who had married Eric II of Norway) and two boys, Alexander and David, had also died before their father. The Scottish state remained intact despite this crisis. Six Guardians were appointed to rule the kingdom on behalf of Alexander's only heir, his 3-year-old granddaughter Margaret, the 'Maid of Norway', the child of his daughter Margaret and Eric of Norway. Consisting of representatives of the Church, the earls and the barons, the most significant act of the Guardians was to negotiate the Treaty of Birgham (1290) with the English King Edward I. This treaty agreed Margaret's betrothal to Edward's son and heir (Edward of Caernarvon, the future Edward II) and confirmed, in that event, the rights and laws of the independent Scottish kingdom as it had existed on 19 March 1286. The intriguing 'what might have been' union between the crowns, three centuries before it actually came about in 1603, came to nought. Margaret survived the tempestuous sea journey from Norway to Scotland, only to die shortly after making landfall in Orkney in September 1290 at the age of seven.

The death of Margaret and failure of the direct royal line left 14 individuals with a claim to the Scottish throne. Within this group, there were two main candidates. These were John Balliol of Barnard Castle and Robert Bruce, Earl of Carrick, both of whom claimed descent from the old royal house and had powerful domestic support. In order to prevent civil war, Edward I was asked by the Guardians to arbitrate between the claimants. Edward I, however, seized his opportunity and insisted that all candidates recognise his status as the overlord of the Scottish kingdom, a status long claimed by the English kings. In practice, this would mean that all Scots were vassals of Edward I, providing him with military service when required. Anyone who was not satisfied with judgements in Scottish royal courts could appeal to Edward and the Scottish Church would also be under the control of English Archbishops. In a legal process known as the Great Cause (1291–2), the majority of the 104 judges chose John Balliol (who did have the better claim in law) and he was inaugurated as King of Scots in November 1292. However, the Scots nobility and church soon chafed at the demands of overlordship, particularly when Edward I demanded Scottish soldiers serve in his wars in Wales and France. The new King John I was forced to appear as a vassal at Edward I's court, and was further undermined when some Scottish claimants, disappointed by the certain rulings of the Scottish High Court, petitioned Edward I instead. By 1295, the Scots had had enough. They sent envoys to make a mutual aid pact with the French king, who was at war with his English counterpart, and prepared for conflict.

The Wars of Independence

ille Princeps Magnificus Rex Anglorum Edwardus...
Regnum nostrum acephalum populumque nullius mali aut
doli conscium nec bellis aut insultibus tunc assuetum
sub amici et confederati specie inimicabiliter infestauit

that mighty prince the King of the English, Edward...
when our kingdom had no head and our people harboured
no malice or treachery and were then unused to wars or invasions,
came in the guise of a friend and ally to harass them as an enemy

The Scottish Wars of Independence lasted from 1296 to 1357 and can be divided into two periods, known as the First (1296–1328) and Second (1332–57) Wars. The wars were made up of two strands. Firstly, attempts by successive English kings to exert their overlordship over Scotland and Scots resistance to these claims. Secondly, and mainly from 1306, a civil war between Balliol and Bruce supporters as both families vied for the throne.

The First War began in 1296 with a Scottish attack on Carlisle. This was followed by an invasion of Scotland by Edward I with a large army. He defeated the Scots at Dunbar, captured King John, stripped him of his title and took Scotland under his direct lordship. Scottish sovereignty was restored following a series of rebellions in 1297 led by William Wallace and Andrew Murray, culminating in a major victory at the Battle of Stirling Bridge on 11 September. Although defeated at Falkirk the following year by an army led by Edward I, Scottish resistance continued until 1304 under a series of leaders acting in the name of the exiled King

John. By 1304, however, the French king had been forced into a treaty with England following a crushing defeat by Flemish townsmen at Courtrai (1302), and the alliance was over. With Edward now able to focus on Scotland, and no help expected from their allies, the majority of the Scottish nobility surrendered. One exception was William Wallace, who was eventually captured and executed in 1305.

The Emergence
of Robert the Bruce

*A quibus Malis innumeris, ipso Juuante qui post
uulnera medetur et sanat, liberati sumus per strenuissimum Principem,
Regem et Dominum nostrum, Dominum Robertum*

**But from these countless evils we have been set free by
our most tireless Prince, King and Lord, the Lord Robert**

In late 1305, Scotland appeared to be a conquered land, but the war was renewed from an unexpected quarter in 1306. This new rebellion was led by Robert Bruce, Earl of Carrick and grandson of the man who had claimed the throne in 1292. Robert seized the throne following the murder of his main rival, John Comyn of Badenoch, in Greyfriars Church at Dumfries. Following early setbacks in 1306–7 and a short spell in exile in the Western Isles or Ireland, Bruce returned to the fray in 1307 and won a series of victories over English garrisons. After the death of Edward I on 7 July, on his way north to quash the rebellion, Bruce was able to take advantage of the domestic troubles of the new English King Edward II, to win a civil war against his Comyn opponents (who supported the Balliol claim) and to cow most of the remaining Scottish nobility into supporting his own claim to the throne. It was 1314 before Edward II was able to mount a major campaign in Scotland, but this ended in disaster for the English army at the Battle of Bannockburn near Stirling on 23 and 24 June. Bruce's forces won a major victory and came close to capturing the English monarch.

After Bannockburn: Famine and Stalemate

*Cuius iniurias, Cedes, violencias, predaciones, incendia,
prelatorum incarceraciones, Monasteriorum combustiones,
Religiosorum spoliaciones et occisiones alia quoque enormia
et innumera que in dicto populo exercuit*

*cruelty, massacre, violence, pillage, arson, imprisoning prelates,
burning down monasteries, robbing and killing monks and nuns,
and yet other outrages without number which he committed
against our people*

While Bannockburn was an important victory, it did not bring English recognition of Bruce's right to the Scottish crown or an end to the war. The years after the battle coincided with a period of particularly severe weather conditions which caused multiple failed harvests, leading to what we now call the Great European Famine (1315–22). This famine caused somewhere in the region of 10–15 per cent mortality rates across large parts of northern Europe. In the same period, a serious disease hit sheep populations, soon followed by the arrival in 1319 of the Bovine Pestilence, a lethal viral disease that led to an 80 per cent mortality rate among cattle. For Scotland, whose economy relied heavily on the export of wool and cow hides, this was a devastating blow, while it was also difficult for either side to force a military victory, leading to a stalemate. During this period, Bruce conducted devastating raids on northern England, and in 1315 opened a second front against the Dublin-based English government in Ireland. This campaign was led by his younger brother, Edward Bruce, who Robert joined with a sizeable force in 1317. Despite early victories, major supply problems, poor weather, famine and disease forced the Scots to retreat. Edward Bruce held on in the north of Ireland until he was defeated and killed at the Battle of Faughart in 1318. Edward was Robert's last surviving brother and had been recognised as his heir by the Scottish nobility in 1315. Although Bruce had been married twice, by 1318 he did not have any surviving children (a son David would be born in 1324). After Edward's death in 1318, his only heir was a grandson, Robert Steward, born in 1316. The death of an adult heir, and of a number of experienced warriors in Ireland, left Bruce in a vulnerable position, which was made more serious by the presence of Edward Balliol at the English court from 1318. Edward was the son of John Balliol, and his heritage and age (he was an adult male in his 30s) made him a viable alternative to Bruce. With English backing, and potential support from any Scots frustrated by a lack of progress since Bannockburn or disillusioned with Robert's kingship, he was a clear threat to the new Bruce dynasty.

This situation may have prompted Bruce to make a statement of his power in early 1318 by attacking the town of Berwick. The town and castle had been in English hands since 1296 and, by attacking and taking both in April 1318, Bruce may have been attempting to reinforce his authority following the problems in Ireland, as well as breaking the stalemate that had existed since 1314. The attack on Berwick, however, broke a truce between the Scots and English that had been declared by Pope John XXII in 1317 and led to Bruce's third excommunication.

Scotland and the Medieval Popes

*Sanctissimo Patri in Christo ac Domino, domino Johanni,
diuina prouidiencia Sacrosauncte Romane
et Vniuersalis Ecclesie Summo Pontifici*

To the most Holy Father and Lord in Christ,
the Lord John, by divine providence Supreme Pontiff
of the Holy Roman and Universal Church

The Bishop of the 'Holy Roman and Universal Church', as the letter termed Pope John XXII, was the undisputed leader of the western Church. Popes did not, at least in the early 14th century, command armies – their most direct weapon was the sentence of excommunication. An excommunicate was excluded from participation in the sacraments and services of the Christian Church, most significantly the Last Sacraments (Confession, Viaticum and Extreme Unction), commonly known as the Last Rites. If imposed on a monarch, excommunication also absolved all subjects of their oaths of allegiance to him – an act of significance for a society where written and verbal oaths were a vital part of the bonds of society. The Papacy also had a number of indirect sources of control and power. They had control over all appointments to benefices, the most lucrative positions in the Church hierarchy, and could use this and other indirect sources of power to influence western European monarchs and leaders to take a course of action they recommended.

From the beginning of the conflict, both the English and the Scots had sought to gain the favour of the Popes. In 1299, Pope

Boniface VIII had ruled that Edward I could not be overlord of Scotland as the kingdom belonged to the Roman See (it enjoyed Special Daughter Status), and in 1301–2 envoys from both kingdoms had presented their sides of the argument at the Papal Curia. By 1305, the new Pope Clément V was less sympathetic to the Scots, concerned primarily with organising a crusade to regain the Holy Land from the Muslims. Internal conflict within and between the Christian kingdoms of western Europe held up such plans. Pope Clément was also faced after 1306 with a Scottish king who had murdered his rival John Comyn on the consecrated soil of Greyfriars Kirk in Dumfries, and had been automatically excommunicated. Although Robert had been briefly absolved from this sentence in 1308 or 1310, he was excommunicated again for the invasion of Ireland in 1315.

The main concern of Pope Clément's successor, Pope John XXII, was also to organise a crusade to reconquer the Holy Land. In this endeavour, the Scots were not expected to play a major role, but Pope John XXII felt that continuing conflict with the Scots prevented the English kings, who had a strong crusading tradition, from taking part. He intervened in the conflict in 1317, sending two Cardinals as envoys to broker a peace. Robert, however, refused to meet these envoys, using the fact that they had not addressed him as King of Scots as a pretext. In addition to the assault on Berwick in 1318, a further raid on northern England in September of 1319, led by two of Bruce's lieutenants, James Douglas and Thomas Randolph, ended with a clash with the Yorkshire militia, led by William Melton, Archbishop of York. A crushing victory for the Scots saw dozens of English clergymen killed or captured. By the autumn of 1319, Papal patience with Bruce and the Scots had been exhausted and Papal Bulls were dispatched summoning Robert and three of his Bishops to appear at Avignon on 1 May 1320 to explain themselves. On 6 January 1320, these were followed by bulls that renewed Robert's excommunication for the murder of John Comyn in 1306.

As we will see, the content and style of the Barons' Letter show that it was both a direct response to this Papal summons, and also to the political threat posed to the fragile Bruce dynasty by the presence of Edward Balliol in northern England.

The Production and Content of the Three Letters

Responding to the Pope

*Barones et Liberetenenetes ac tota Communitas Regni Scocie,
omnimodam Reuerenciam filialem*

**barons and freeholders of the whole community of the realm
send all manner of filial reverence**

A common misconception surrounding the Declaration of Arbroath is that it was drafted by the barons who signed it at a parliament held in Arbroath in April of 1320. This traditional view is depicted in murals at Arbroath Railway Station and has been acted out in pageants that have been held in the town to mark anniversaries of the document. These images and plays show large numbers of hairy and heavily armed Scottish noblemen gathering to sign this momentous document. This was not the case. The Barons' Letter was not issued by a parliament, it was the product of the royal administration of Robert 1, although the barons in whose names it was sent would have been expected to be in general agreement with its content and sentiments.

The decision to respond to the summons to Avignon seems to have been taken by Robert and his advisors in late 1319 or early 1320. This response would consist of three letters. The others, from the King and from the Scottish clergy, have not survived, although we know of their existence through the Papal letters that responded to them. A rough idea of the content of the letters from Robert and the clergy can be surmised by these Papal responses, and from similar letters sent in 1309. These are included alongside the Barons' Letter later in this book.

Bruce summoned a full council to meet at the Cistercian Monastery of Newbattle Abbey, not far from Edinburgh, in March 1320. The main purpose of this meeting was clearly to gain the consent of major barons and clergy for the content of the two letters due to be sent to the Pope in their name, accompanied by a third from the King himself. At Newbattle, and over the following weeks, the seals of 39 barons were attached to the letter in preparation for its dispatch, with a group of diplomats, to Avignon. The final copies of the letters were dated 6 April 1320 and addressed from Arbroath Abbey, the location of the royal chancery. The chancery was the writing office that was responsible for the production of royal documents, such as diplomatic letters, and it was headed by Bernard of Kilwinning. Bernard, who had been Robert's chancellor since 1308 and abbot of Arbroath since 1310, has traditionally been identified as the author of the letter. However, unlike most of the high-ranking churchmen, he lacked a university degree, and as it was unusual for chancellors to actually write such documents, it is unlikely he was directly responsible for the wording of the Barons' Letter. Several other candidates have been put forward, most notably Alexander Kininmouth, later Bishop of Aberdeen, and Walter Twynholm, who succeeded Bernard as chancellor in 1328. In fact, it is unlikely to have been the effort of an individual, but of a team of writers either from Abbot Bernard's chancery or in the employ of the Bishop of St Andrews, William Lamberton.

It is clear from the content and style of the Barons' Letter that the author or authors knew their stuff. It uses the Papal cursus (a writing style popular at the Papal Curia), is heavily laced with biblical references and includes a classical quotation from Sallust, a Roman writer of the 1st century BCE. It was therefore intended to impress its Papal audience and was composed by diplomatically trained and highly educated men. As a petition to the Papacy, it built on several recent precedents and the writer(s) were clearly familiar with earlier examples of this style of document. As well as echoing earlier charters of liberties like the Magna Carta (1215), it was of a similar style to a document from 1317 known as the 'Remonstrances of the Irish Princes'. The author(s) also appear to have had access to, or been aware of, similar appeals to the Papacy from kings and barons, such as one sent by Edward I and his barons in 1301, and one from the French nobility sent to Pope Boniface VIII in 1302.

The Barons' Letter, and presumably the letter from the clergy, also leant heavily on materials that had been used in the propaganda war of earlier stages of the independence struggles of the Scots. In particular, it includes similar arguments to those made by a Scottish embassy to the Papacy in 1301, the main points of which have been preserved in a 15th-century chronicle. This embassy – led by a man called Master Baldred Bisset – used earlier sources such as the history of the kingdom written in the 1260s, to refute English claims to overlordship over Scotland. The Barons' Letter also used these earlier materials, and arguments made in two earlier letters sent from Scotland to King Philip IV of France in 1309, known as Declarations of the Scottish Clergy and Nobility. The brilliance of the Barons' Letter was that it provided a superbly concise and coherent articulation of the arguments for Scottish sovereignty made in these early documents, and did so in a diplomatic style that would have been guaranteed to have the greatest impact with its Papal audience.

The Content
of the Barons' Letter

The letter produced in 1320 was divided into ten core sections. Each of these had a part to play in persuading the Pope to lift the sentence of excommunication, recognise Robert as the legitimate King of Scots and use his influence to force the English King to do likewise. It began with a formal address to the Pope and a list of the major noblemen of Scotland, the men whom the letter claimed to be from. The list included eight of the earls, the most senior noblemen, and 31 of the major barons before, in a sweeping statement, referring to the consent of 'the rest of the barons and freeholders, and whole community, of the kingdom of Scotland'. While this phrase could be taken to imply that the letter was in essence a petition with mass support, rather like the National Covenant of the 1630s, which was signed and witnessed by several thousand Scots, it meant something different in a 14th-century context. The 'community' referred to the political community, the small group of men, and sometimes women, of noble birth who were the major landowners and political power brokers in medieval states. It is unlikely that it was intended to refer to the people of the burghs, or the mass of the population who lived and worked in the countryside, groups who had a very limited role in politics in the middle ages.

The second and third sections laid out a concise history of the kingdom of the Scots. It traced the movement of the 'nation' from Greater Scythia to Scotland via Spain, and their governance since their arrival in Scotland by a succession of 113 kings, none of whom, it claims, were of foreign stock. For a modern audience, this mythical origin story is the most challenging section of the letter, including as it does a number of obvious fictions, such as the claim that the Picts were driven out by the Scots on their arrival in what is now Scotland (the two groups co-existed as neighbours for several centuries). However, by the 14th century, all major medieval states had developed similar origin stories that pushed the independence of their kingdom as far back as possible into the past, preferably into antiquity. For example, in what is known as the Brut legends, the origins of the kingdom of England were traced to refugees from the fall of Troy, while the French kings traced their ancestry to the founders of Rome.

Versions of the Scottish legend presented in the Barons' Letter can be seen in the diplomatic documents of 1301, in the history of the kingdom written in the 1260s, and in earlier king-lists from the 12th and 13th centuries. These early versions were brilliantly condensed into a few lines in the letter of 1320. It let the Papal audience know in no uncertain terms that Scotland was a proper, long established kingdom that had never been subject to another, clearly refuting English claims to overlordship. The following paragraph took this argument further by reminding the Pope that the patron saint of Scotland was none other than the apostle St Andrew. The arrival of his relics in Scotland was used to further evidence the divine blessing of the Scots, but also cleverly reminded the Pope of the close connections between the kingdom and the Papacy. St Andrew was the brother of St Peter, whose relics were found in Rome and who was considered the founder of the western Church. In the opening section of the fourth paragraph, it also reminded the Pope that his predecessors had recognised the sovereignty of the kingdom by granting its Church a special status, subtly referring to Pope Boniface VII's ruling of 1299 that Edward I could not be overlord of Scotland as the kingdom was under the special protection of the Roman See.

In the fourth and fifth sections, the letter delved into some more recent history, providing an account of the wars and of the reign of Robert I from a decidedly Scottish perspective. It put the blame for the conflict firmly at the door of Edward I, accusing him of a range of atrocities, a number of which it claims were perpetrated against churchmen and Church property, something clearly intended to chime with the Papal audience. Liberty was restored by the emergence of Robert, who they compare to Old Testament military leaders, Joshua and Judas Maccabeus. The letter justified Robert's usurpation of the throne by stating that his military victories indicated divine providence for this rule, that he had a legal right to the throne and that he had assumed the crown with assent of 'all the people'. The final two points were generous with the truth: John Balliol had a better claim in 1292 and Bruce had fought a long and bitter civil war with Balliol supporters after 1306 to secure the throne. In 1320, Edward Balliol was across the border, as were many Scottish exiles who opposed the Bruce dynasty.

This version of events from 1296–1320 was followed by the most quoted section of the letter, known as the 'deposition clause' by historians. In a few fascinating lines, the authors of the letter state that should Bruce, or any of his successors, consent to English overlordship, the Scottish nobility would replace him with another king who was prepared to protect these freedoms – 'for, as long as a hundred of us remain alive, never will we on any conditions be subjected to the lordship of the English'. This was followed by the line taken from Roman Historian Sallust's *De Catilinae coniuratione* (the Catiline Conspiracy to overthrow the Roman Republic in 63 BCE),

'It is in truth not for glory, nor riches, nor honours that we are fighting, but for freedom alone, which no honest man gives up but with life itself'. Popular discussion of the letter has tended to take this section at face value, using it to argue that the Scots practised some form of contractual kingship. Akin to an early form of democracy, the kings were considered to derive their right to rule from the consent of 'the people', thus making them unique in medieval Europe, or anywhere else for that matter until the modern era. Historians tend to discount this idea, as there is no evidence of the idea of contractual kingship being discussed, or in any way ratified, in Scotland in the centuries before or after 1320.

The main debate among historians regards the constitutional significance of this section, but more recent works have stressed that, in the context of 1320, it had two main aims. Firstly, it justified the deposition of John 1 (Balliol), a man who is not named in the letter, but who hovers behind the text. Secondly, it provided a warning to those who would consider supporting the restoration of his son, Edward Balliol, who, as we have seen, was in northern England from 1318. Any restoration of the Balliol dynasty could only happen with English military support, and presumably with an acknowledgement of English overlordship (as would actually happen in 1332–3). The deposition clause warned its audience, both in Scotland and beyond, that the Bruce dynasty was prepared to go to any lengths to avoid the return of Balliol, to the extent of finding another adult male to replace Robert should he die without further heirs.

With the close of section six and the quote from Sallust, the author(s) of the letter must have felt that the case for the sovereignty of the kingdom, and for Robert's right to the throne, had been made, for in the remainder of the letter there was a distinct change of tone as the author places the ball firmly in the Papal court. The seventh and eighth sections urged the Pope to use his influence to force the English King to put an end to the conflict. If he did this, the Scots, and the English King it was implied, would happily join the Pope's plan for a crusade to the Holy Land. In the ninth section, the tone became a little more combative, warning the Pope against putting too much faith in English claims, in which case the blame for further bloodshed would be at his door. It finished with a more polite repetition of the Scots submission to John's authority.

In a relatively short letter, it provided a direct and uncomplicated refutation of the English Crown's claims to overlordship over Scotland, urges the Pope to lift the sentence of excommunication, to recognise Robert as legitimate King of Scots and to persuade the English King, Edward II, to do the same. If he took heed, it argued, John's long-planned crusade can become a reality. It is a triumph of tone, conciseness and of understanding your target audience.

SECTION III

The Impact and Significance of the Barons' Letter since 1320

The Reception of the Letters
and the End of the War

There is no direct evidence of the weather conditions when the letters were produced in March/April 1320 or those the Scottish emissaries faced as they made the long journey to Avignon by land and sea. Cold and wet was the long-term trend from the latter part of the 13th century. However, as with today when the breaking of rainfall or temperature records is the norm from year to year, unseasonably warm or freezing conditions were equally possible. Unpredictable weather was the challenge of the early years of the Little Ice Age. The much-improved harvests of 1318 and 1319 (compared to the bad years of 1315–7) suggest more settled conditions, but the Bovine Pestilence that arrived in Scotland in 1319 and lingered until 1321–2 would have limited the recovery. The context for the delivery of the three letters to Avignon in the summer of 1320 was therefore of a Bruce regime keen to break a political and military deadlock, in the midst of an environmental crisis.

The exact date that the diplomatic mission carrying the letters arrived in Avignon has not survived, but it must have been sometime between 16 June, when Papal Bulls were issued excommunicating Bruce and the Bishops for not arriving by the 1 May deadline, and 16 August when Papal replies to the letters are recorded. The letters and embassy had an immediate impact. After considering their content, the Pope placed the sentences of excommunication on hold until 1 April 1321, while in a further bull sent on 28 August, the Pope told the barons that he had communicated with Edward II, urging him to engage in peace negotiations with the Scots. In letters sent to the English King, he referred to Robert as 'King of Scotland' and quoted passages from the letters. In terms of their aims, the letters and envoys had succeeded in getting the sentence of excommunication lifted (or suspended at least), gained a recognition of Bruce's kingship and persuaded the Pope to put pressure on Edward II to come to the table for peace negotiations. In helping to reach peaceful settlement of the Wars of Independence, the letters and arguments of the envoys were, however, only a qualified success.

The peace negotiations that resulted from the diplomacy of 1320 were a failure. Papal pressure did encourage peace talks, which took place at Bamburgh in northern England in 1321, although the Bovine Pestilence and generally dire environmental conditions of the early 1320s may also have played a role in persuading both sides to take a break from warfare. The talks were a failure, and conflict resumed in 1322. It would take a major Scottish victory at the Battle of Old Byland in Yorkshire in October 1322, at which the English King again only narrowly avoided capture, to begin peace talks and an 11-year truce was agreed in May 1323. The First Wars of Independence finally ended, only after a palace coup in England in 1327 saw Edward II deposed and killed by his wife Isabella and her partner Roger Mortimer. It was their short-lived regime that negotiated the Treaty of Edinburgh-Northampton in 1328, by which they recognised the independence of the kingdom of the Scots and the legitimacy of the Bruce dynasty. Shortly after this, in June 1329, Robert I died at Cardross in Dunbartonshire

When Edward III in turn removed the Mortimer regime and took power in England, he did not feel bound by the treaty and warfare resumed in 1332. The Second Wars of Independence began with the return of Edward Balliol, supported by an army of both English and Scots who had been disinherited by the Bruces. Balliol was initially successful, defeating supporters of Robert's son and successor David II and forcing the young King into exile. Balliol had himself crowned King at Scone in September 1332, but was increasingly reliant on English support from 1333. In the years that followed, a combination of fierce resistance from supporters of the Bruce dynasty and the distraction of the Hundred Years' War, which began in 1337, saw English enthusiasm for the conflict wane. The Bruce supporters regained the ascendancy and by 1341 it was safe for the 17-year King David II to return. It would be the defeat and capture of David II at the Battle of Neville's Cross in 1346 that would ultimately bring an end to the war. Balliol, by then a figure with little support in Scotland, formally surrendered his claim to the throne to Edward III in 1356. The English King made several offers to release David II from captivity in return for a recognition of his overlordship but was rebuffed by the Scottish nobles. David II was eventually ransomed in 1357 without any such precondition and the Wars of Independence came to an end.

The Long-term Significance
of the Barons' Letter
in Scotland

I ronically, it was in the latter part of the reign of David II that the
deposition clause of the Barons' Letter was put to the test.
David II, childless from his first marriage, presented a plan to
Parliament in 1363 that would allow a younger son of Edward III to
be named as his successor. While the letter itself was never directly
mentioned in the frank discussions that followed this plan, some
historians have felt that its influence can be seen in the arguments
made by David II's opponents, who ultimately defeated the plan.
This is fairly typical of the quest for significance of the letter in the
three centuries that followed its production, where direct evidence
for the influence of its text and ideas are difficult to find. While it
has been stated that it was unknown in Scotland until the 17th
century, that is not strictly true. The letter was included in several
Scottish Chronicles from the late 14th and 15th centuries and
seems to have been reasonably well-known. A number of the key
themes – freedom and loyalty to a king, as well as the right to resist
tyranny – were explored by Scottish writers in the 15th and 16th
centuries, but none of them specifically referenced or directly
quoted it. It would be fair to say that evidence for its significance
during the remainder of the middle ages and early modern period
is difficult to find.

This changed from the 1680s. The Barons' Letter was published
by itself for the first time in 1689, with an accompanying translation

from Latin into English. It had been used by several writers in political tracts earlier that decade, and from 1689–1707 it was cited by a range of authors to justify the deposition of James VII and II in 1689 in relation to the Darien Scheme (1698–1700) and by both sides in the debates surrounding the Act of Union of 1707. It was reprinted and quoted on several occasions in the first half of the 18th century by Jacobites, who in 1715, 1719 and 1745–6 raised rebellions in support of the restoration of the descendants of the deposed Stuart King James VII. In the latter part of the century, the association with Arbroath first seems to have brought the picturesque ruins of the abbey on to the tourist itinerary, when Thomas Pennant, James Boswell and Dr Johnson visited the site and commented on its connections to the text. The letter was mentioned briefly in historical and fictional works by Walter Scott and others in the 19th century and in 1904 a local historian, J Brodie, first used the term Declaration when referring to the text. Since this was repeated in *The Source Book of Scottish History* in 1952, it has universally become known as the Declaration of Arbroath.

While groups on the fringes of the nationalist movement in Scotland in the latter part of the 20th century have made regular use of the letter, mainstream political parties have tended to be wary of engaging with it and there has been some criticism in the media of the lack of official events being held by Scottish Government to mark the 700-year anniversary in 2020. It is the Scottish Claim of Right of 1689, itself with connections to the Barons' Letter, that has provided a focus for politicians interested in devolution or independence since the 1980s.

In 1988–9, a new Scottish Claim of Right, deliberately echoing the 1689 document, was published by a cross-party group of Labour, Liberal Democrat and Scottish National Party MPs, calling for a constitutional convention and for a referendum on devolution. Following the victory of the Labour Party at the 1997 UK election, a referendum was held in Scotland in which people voted for devolution, establishing the Scottish Parliament that opened in 1999 and transferring some of the powers previously held at Westminster. The idea of a further Scottish Claim of Right was revived in 2012 by the Scottish National Party, this time in support of independence via a referendum, which took place in September 2014. The referendum saw the Scottish people vote against independence and, since 2016 and most recently in a speech by the current First Minister in January 2020, there have been further calls by politicians in Scotland who support a second referendum for a new Claim of Right and a constitutional assembly to discuss Scotland's future. Like the Barons' Letter that was one of its inspirations, the Scottish Claim of Right of 1689 has proved to have an enduring appeal for groups across the political spectrum in Scotland.

The Barons' Letter
and the
Declaration of Independence

When Senate Resolution 155 (20 March 1998) officially designated 6 April as Tartan Day, it reflected an increasingly common assertion in the United States that the letter, which the resolution erroneously referred to as Scotland's Declaration of Independence, had a direct influence on their own Declaration of Independence of 1776. This view can also now be commonly found in popular works and in internet-based references to the document in Scotland as well. Aside from the use of the word Declaration (which as we have seen was not used to describe the Scottish document until the 20th century), there are three elements to the argument in favour of a connection between the two. Firstly, there is a strong tradition of freedom and popular sovereignty in Scotland that was expressed most clearly in the letter of 1320, which can be seen in the language and sentiments of the Declaration of Independence. Secondly, a number of Scots played a part in drawing up the 1776 document. Most notably among the signatories were John Witherspoon and James Wilson, who had been born and educated in Scotland before they emigrated to the American Colonies. While neither of these men are known to have cited or referred to the letter directly, in their published works they drew on a long tradition of Scottish political thought. These included the ideas of the 17th-century Covenanters and arguments in favour of the deposition of James VII in 1689, known as the Scottish Claim of Right.

The final element of the argument is that the Scots must have influenced the document, as a significant number of men of Scottish descent, including Thomas Jefferson, were involved in the drafting of the Declaration of Independence and in the wider debates around the subject in the 1760s and 1770s. Jefferson appears to have been influenced by the English Declaration of Rights of 1689, which, like the Scottish Claim of Right, argued in favour of the deposition of James VII and II, and used similar language to both in the Declaration. It is clear then that the Declaration of Independence was influenced in part by Scottish documents like the Claim of Right, which was part of a tradition of political thought that included the Barons' Letter. While there is no definitive evidence of a direct connection between the two documents, it would be wrong to suggest that there is no link between them at all.

Recent Historical Controversies and Debates

The connections between the letter and the United States Declaration of Independence have been explored at length by Scottish historians, with most expressing caution in directly linking the two documents. That debate is one of a number concerning the letter that have emerged since the 1960s when it became an object of serious study by scholars. Fifty years of research by GWS Barrow, AAM Duncan, Grant G Simpson, and more recently Edward J Cowan and Michael Penman, amongst others, has overturned many of the myths concerning the document's production. They have also explored the context in which it was written and provided a detailed understanding of the content, the main conclusions of which are included in this book. Significant debates still remain, however, as to whether it can be viewed as an expression of Scottish nationalism, with opinion divided as to the relevance of terms like nationalism in a medieval context. In particular, there are disagreements over the interpretation of the meaning of the term freedom as expressed in 1320. Did it refer to national or personal freedom? There are also disputes over its political and constitutional significance in the centuries following its production. Should we take the 'deposition clause' seriously as an indication of a constitutional relationship between the Scottish kings and their subjects, or was it merely rhetoric? Why was it so rarely cited and quoted after 1320, or was it such a well-known text that it was unnecessary to do so? The fascination of history as a discipline is such that debates will continue as the 700th anniversary stimulates a renewed interest in what is known as the Declaration of Arbroath, as recent films have done with the Wars of Independence more generally, and that older, and newer, scholars will bring new ideas and views to the discussion of the document.

CONCLUSION

The Declaration of Arbroath: What it meant then and what it means now

This book has aimed to address a series of questions about how we should read and understand the letter we now call the Declaration of Arbroath. Should it be read as a seminal statement of Scottish national identity or is it best understood as a practical response to a diplomatic problem? Was it the model for the United States Declaration of Independence or a clever piece of medieval rhetoric? Does it provide evidence for the strength of support for the 'hero king' Robert the Bruce or for the weakness of his usurping regime?

We should be cautious in making a direct connection between the document produced in 1320 and the United States Declaration of Independence of 1776, but not rule out an indirect influence. Rather than a clear vote of support for King Robert, the letter was borne of the difficult political and environmental situation faced by the Scots and the precarious position of the fledgling Bruce dynasty in 1319–20. The three letters sent to the Pope in 1320 were a practical and, ultimately, effective, response to this difficult situation and to a pressing diplomatic problem. It is unlikely, however, that the author(s) intended to produce a statement of national identity for the ages. In attempting to resolve the problems posed by the Papal Bulls of 1319, they drew upon western European political theory and upon 30 years or more of Scottish arguments for the sovereignty of their kingdom, to produce a remarkable letter whose memorable language and core themes of resistance to tyranny and popular sovereignty continue to have relevance for those who read it today.

While questions remain regarding the content of the letter, its continued significance, particularly from the 1680s, is one area that is not under debate. From the late seventeenth century, the Barons' Letter began to assume an importance for Scots from a range of political backgrounds, and has done so ever since. The themes discussed in the letter – defiance of tyranny, freedom and resistance to foreign rule – have appealed to those from every shade of political opinion. It was in the second half of the 20th century that the letter and its contents appear to have had a wider impact on the public consciousness. Celebrations of the 650th anniversary of the document in 1970, which included a commemorative stamp produced by the Post Office and events held at Arbroath, contributed to this appreciation of the document by the general public. The 700th anniversary is being marked in Scotland's capital by a collaboration between the National Museum of Scotland, who are putting the letter on display, and the National Records of Scotland where a series of talks will be held. For academics, there will be a major international conference, held appropriately at Newbattle Abbey in April 2020. In Arbroath, the anniversary will be marked by a procession through the town and a range of other cultural events. Further afield, in Australia, 2020 has been designated the 'Year of Scotland', with 6 April marked by a pageant held at the Centennial Parklands in Glen Innes, New South Wales, while the connections between the document and the Declaration of Independence are set to be a key theme of the 2020 Tartan Day celebrations in New York City.

The author(s) of the Papal petition of 1320 would probably have been greatly surprised to find that, 700 years later, their work and their words would continue to be celebrated and considered so significant. Like us, they were grappling with the challenges posed by climate change and political uncertainty, but in most other respects the distance in time means that they lived in a different world to their modern readers. Under the guidance of a strong and ruthless monarch, they had drafted letters to the Pope with specific goals in mind, and it is much to the credit of their rhetorical and diplomatic skills that the sentiments they expressed in what we now know as the Declaration of Arbroath still resonate so strongly today.

The Other Letters from 1320

Robert I's Cover Letter

The contents of Robert I's 'cover' letter can be pieced together from two surviving Papal responses to it, dated 16 and 28 August 1320. While the Barons' Letter dealt with broad questions, like the sovereignty of the Scottish kingdom, Robert I's letter addressed three specific issues. Firstly, he repeated complaints that had been made regularly in correspondence with the Pope and his envoys since 1317 that they had failed to address him as the King of Scots. Earlier correspondence addressed Bruce as the governor of Scotland, or the man who calls himself King. The second issue addressed in the letter was a long running dispute over who should be the Bishop of Glasgow. Robert I complained that the Pope had been obstructing his chosen candidates since 1316, when the last Bishop, Robert Wishart, had died. Robert I's initial chosen successor was a man called Stephen of Dunnideer, but he was rejected by the Pope under pressure from Edward II, and died on his way home from Avignon. Robert I's next candidate, John Lindsay, was also rejected by the Pope, who consecrated Edward II's candidate John of Eggliscliffe instead. This English-backed Bishop never set foot in Scotland, and John Lindsay was finally successfully appointed to the See in 1323. Robert probably also repeated the claims found in the letters from the clergy and barons that it was the actions of the English King that prevented peace and his personal involvement in crusade. Robert I may also have suggested that the Pope appoint a date and time for peace talks between himself and Edward II, as he appears to have sent a letter to the English King around this time offering such talks. The remainder of the letter seems to have involved the King declaring his general support for the Scottish Church and its clergy, and personally requesting that the Pope relax his sentence of excommunication.

The Letter from the Clergy

We can recreate the likely content of the Letter from the Clergy from the similar document sent to Philip IV of France in 1309, and notes that survive from the arguments made by the Scottish embassy to the Pope in 1301. The Declaration of the Clergy, sent to the French King in 1309, was mainly concerned with stressing the Scottish Church's support for Robert I and accounting for the deposition of John Balliol. It argued that in 1292, Robert I (the current King's grandfather) was actually the true heir of Alexander III, and that John been made King only at the behest of Edward I. Thereafter, he was deprived of the throne by Edward, and therefore Robert's seizure of the crown in 1306 was legitimate. A central part of the argument presented by the Scottish embassy to the Papacy in 1301, was the claim that Christianity had been brought to Scotland in the 4th century by the arrival of the relics of St Andrew. The conversion of the Scots was therefore said to have occurred before the 'English' had embraced the faith, and the connection between Rome and Scotland was also claimed to be of longer duration than that with the southern neighbour.

The 1320 version would have been drafted by the same men as the Barons' Letter and was therefore almost certainly a condensed and improved version of the arguments of 1301 and the letter of 1309. Like the Barons' Letter, it was almost certainly filled with a range of biblical and legal precedents for their support for Robert I. It would have expanded on the section in the Barons' Letter that argued for the early conversion of the Scots to Christianity and provided some further detail on the 1,000-year history of the Scottish Church that followed. It may well have claimed, as later histories of the Scots would, that it was missionary work of

Scottish saints like Ninian, Columba and Aidan that had converted the Saxons of northern England. For the Scots, the long-term independence of the Scottish Church and the patronage of St Andrew were, alongside the long list of kings, important elements of their argument for the sovereignty of the kingdom.

The Declaration of Arbroath in Latin

Sanctissimo Patri in Christo ac Domino, domino Johanni, diuina prouidiencia Sacrosauncte Romane et Vniuersalis Ecclesie Summo Pontifici, Filii Sui Humiles et deuoti Duncanus Comes de Fyf, Thomas Ranulphi Comes Morauie Dominus Mannie et Vallis Anandie, Patricius de Dumbar Comes Marchie, Malisius Comes de Stratheryne, Malcolmus Comes de Leuenax, Willelmus Comes de Ross, Magnus Comes Cathanie et Orkadie et Willelmus Comes Suthirlandie; Walterus Senescallus Scocie, Willelmus de Soules Buttelarius Scocie, Jacobus Dominus de Duglas, Rogerus de Moubray, Dauid Dominus de Brechyn, Dauid de Graham, Ingeramus de Vmfrauille, Johannes de Menetethe Custos Comitatus de Menetethe, Alexander Fraser, Gilbertus de Haya Constabularius Scocie, Robertus de Keth Marescallus Scocie, Henricus de Sancto Claro, Johannes de Graham, Dauid de Lindesay, Willelmus Olifaunt, Patricius de Graham, Johannes de Fentoun, Willelmus de Abirnithy, Dauid de Wemys, Willelmus de Montefixo, Fergusius de Ardrossane, Eustachius de Maxwell, Willelmus de Ramesay, Willelmus de Montealto, Alanus de Morauia, Douenaldus Cambell, Johannes Cambrun, Reginaldus le chen, Alexander de Setoun, Andreas de Lescelyne, et Alexander de Stratoun, Ceterique Barones et Liberetenenetes ac tota Communitas Regni Scocie, omnimodam Reuerenciam filialem cum deuotis Pedum osculis beatorum.

Scimus, Sanctissime Pater et Domine, et ex antiquorum gestis et libris Colligimus quod inter Ceteras naciones egregias nostra scilicet Scottorum nacio multis preconijs fuerit insignita, que de Maiori Schithia per Mare tirenum et Columpnas Herculis transiens et in Hispania inter ferocissimas gentes per multa temporum curricula Residens a nullis quantumcumque barbaricis poterat allicubi gentibus subiugari. Indeque veniens post mille et ducentos annos a transitu populi israelitici per mare rubrum sibi sedes in Occidente quas nunc optinet, expulsis primo Britonibus et Pictis omnino deletis, licet per Norwagienses, Dacos et Anglicos sepius inpugnata fuerit, multis cum victorijs et Laboribus quamplurimis adquisuit, ipsaque ab omni seruitute liberas, vt Priscorum testantur Historie, semper tenuit. In quorum Regno Centum et Tredescim Reges de ipsorum Regali prosapia, nullo alienigena interueniente, Regnauerunt.

Quorum Nobilitates et Merita, licet ex aliis non clarerent, satis patenter effulgent ex eo quod Rex Regum et dominancium dominus Jhesus Christus post passionem suam et Resurreccionem ipsos in vltimis terre finibus constitutos quasi primos ad suam fidem sanctissimam conuocauit. Nec eos per quemlibet in dicta fide confirmari voluit set per suum primum apostolum vocacione quamuis ordine secundum vel tercium, sanctum Andream mitissimum beati Petri Germanum, quem semper ipsis preesse voluit vt Patronum. Hec autem Sanctissimi Patres et Predecessores vestri sollicita mente pensantes ipsum Regnum et populum vt beati Petri germani peculium multis fauoribus et priuilegijs quamplurimis Munierunt, Ita quippe quod gens nostra sub ipsorum proteccione hactenus libera deguit et quieta donec ille Princeps Magnificus Rex Anglorum Edwardus, pater istius qui nunc est, Regnum nostrum acephalum populumque nullius mali aut doli conscium nec bellis aut insultibus tunc assuetum sub amici et confederati specie inimicabiliter infestauit. Cuius iniurias, Cedes, violencias, predaciones, incendia, prelatorum incarceraciones, Monasteriorum combustiones, Religiosorum spoliaciones et occisiones alia quoque enormia et innumera que in dicto populo exercuit, nulli parcens etati aut sexui, Religioni aut ordini, nullus scriberet nec ad plenum intelligeret nisi quem experiencia informaret.

A quibus Malis innumeris, ipso Juuante qui post uulnera medetur et sanat, liberati sumus per strenuissimum Principem, Regem et Dominum nostrum, Dominum Robertum, qui pro populo et hereditate suis de manibus Inimicorum liberandis quasi alter Machabeus aut Josue labores et tedia, inedias et pericula, leto sustinuit animo. Quem eciam diuina disposicio et iuxta leges et Consuetudines nostra, quas vsque ad mortem sustinere volumus, Juris successio et debitus nostrorum omnium Consensus et Assensus nostrum fecerunt Principem atque Regem, cui tanquam illi per quem salus in populo nostro facta est pro nostra libertate tuenda tam Jure quam meritis tenemur et volumus in omnibus adherere.

Quem si ab inceptis desisteret, Regi Anglorum aut Anglicis nos aut Regnum nostrum volens subicere, tanquam Inimicum nostrum et sui nostrique Juris subuersorem statim expellere niteremur et alium Regem nostrum qui ad defensionem nostram sufficeret faceremus. Quia quamdiu Centum ex nobis viui remanserint, nuncquam Anglorum dominio aliquatenus volumus subiugari. Non enim propter gloriam, diuicias aut honores pugnamus set propter libertatem solummodo quam Nemo bonus nisi simul cum vita amittit.

Hinc est, Reuerende Pater et Domine, quod sanctitatem vestram omni precum instancia genuflexis cordibus exoramus quatinus sincero corde Menteque pia recensentes quod apud eum cuius vices in terris geritis cum non sit Pondus nec distinccio Judei et greci, Scoti aut Anglici, tribulaciones et angustias nobis et Ecclesie dei illatas ab Anglicis paternis occulis intuentes, Regem Anglorum, cui sufficere debet quod possidet cum olim Anglia septem aut pluribus solebat sufficere Regibus, Monere et exhortari dignemini vt nos scotos, in exili degentes Scocia vltra quam habitacio non est nichilque nisi nostrum Cupientes, in pace dimittat. Cui pro nostra procuranda quiete quicquid possumus, ad statum nostrum Respectu habito, facere volumus cum effectu.

Vestra enim interest, sancte Pater, hoc facere qui paganorum feritatem, Christianorum culpis exigentibus, in Christianos seuientem aspicitis et Christianorum terminos arctari indies, quantumque vestre sanctitatis memorie derogat si (quod absit) Ecclesia in aliqua sui parte vestris temporibus patiatur eclipsim aut Scandalum, vos videritis. Excitet igitur Christianos Principes qui non causam vt causam ponentes se fingunt in subsidium terre sancte propter guerras quas habent cum proximis ire non posse. Cuius inpedimenti Causa est verior quod in Minoribus proximis debellandis vtilitas propior et resistencia debilior estimantur. Set quam leto corde dictus dominus Rex noster et Nos si Rex Anglorum nos in pace dimitteret illuc iremus qui nichil ignorat satis novit. Quod Christi vicario totique Christianitati ostendimus et testamur.

Quibus si sanctitas vestra Anglorum relatibus nimis credula fidem sinceram non adhibeat aut ipsis in nostram confusionem fauere non desinat, corporum excidia, animarum exicia, et cetera que sequentur incomoda que ipsi in nobis et Nos in ipsis fecerimus vobis ab altissimo credimus inputanda.

Ex quo sumus et erimus in hiis que tenemur tanquam obediencie filii vobis tanquam ipsius vicario parati in omnibus complacere, ipsique tanquam Summo Regi et Judici causam nostram tuendam committimus, Cogitatum nostrum Jactantes in ipso sperantesque firmiter quod in nobis virtutem faciet et ad nichilum rediget hostes nostros. Sanctitatem ac sanitatem vestram conseruet altissimus Ecclesie sue sancte per tempora diuturna.

Datum apud Monasterium de Abirbrothoc in Scocia sexto die mensis Aprilis Anno gracie Millesimo Trescentesimo vicesimo Anno vero Regni Regis nostri supradicti Quinto decimo.

Endorsed: Littere directe ad dominum Supremum Pontificem per communitatem Scocie.

The Declaration of Arbroath in English

To the most Holy Father and Lord in Christ, the Lord John, by divine providence Supreme Pontiff of the Holy Roman and Universal Church, his humble and devout sons Duncan, Earl of Fife, Thomas Randolph, Earl of Moray, Lord of Man and Annandale, Patrick Dunbar, Ealrl of March, Malise, Earl of Strathearn, Malcolm, Earl of Lennox, William, Earl of Ross, Magnus, Earl of Caithness and Orkney and William, Earl of Sutherland; Walter, Steward of Scotland, William Soules, Butler of Scotland, James Lord of Douglas, Roger Mowbray, David, Lord of Brechin, David Graham, Ingram Umfraville,, John Menteith, Guardian of the earldom of Menteith, Alexander Fraser, Gilbert Hay, Constable of Scotland, Robert Keith, Marischal of Scotland, Henry St Clair, John Graham, David Lindsay, William Oliphant, Patrick Graham, John Fenton, William Abernethy, David Wemyss, William Mushet, Fergus of Ardrossan, Eustace Maxwell, William Ramsay, William Mowat, Alan Murray, Donald Campbell, John Cameron, Reginald Cheyne, Alexander Seton, Andrew Leslie and Alexander of Straiton, and the other barons and freeholders of the whole community of the realm of Scotland send all manner of filial reverence, with devout kisses of his blessed feet.

Most Holy Father and Lord, we know and from the chronicles and books of the ancients we find that among other famous nations our own, the Scots, have been graced with widespread renown. They journeyed from Greater Scythia by way of the Tyrrhenian Sea and the Pillars of Hercules, and dwelt for a long course of time in Spain among the most savage tribes, but nowhere could they be subdued by any race, however barbarous. Thence they came, twelve hundred years after the people of Israel crossed the Red Sea, to their home in the west where they still live today. The Britons they first drove out, the Picts they utterly destroyed, and, even though very often assailed by the Norwegians, the Danes and the English, they took possession of that home with many victories and untold efforts; and, as the historians of old time bear witness, they have held it free of all bondage ever since. In their kingdom there have reigned one hundred and thirteen kings of their own royal stock, the line unbroken by a single foreigner.

The high qualities and deserts of these people, were they not otherwise manifest, gain glory enough from this; that the King of kings and Lord of lords, our Lord Jesus Christ, after his Passion and Resurrection, called them, even though settled in the uttermost parts of the earth, almost the first to His most holy faith. Nor would He have them confirmed in that faith by merely anyone but by the first of His Apostles – by calling, though second or third in rank – the most gentle Saint Andrew, the Blessed Peter's brother, and desired him to keep them under his protection as their patron forever.

The Most Holy Fathers your predecessors gave careful heed to these things and bestowed many favours and numerous privileges on this same kingdom and people, as being the special charge of the Blessed Peter's brother. Thus our nation under their protection did indeed live in freedom and peace up to the time when that mighty prince the king of the English, Edward, the father of the one who reigns today, when our kingdom had no head and our people harboured no malice or treachery and were then unused to wars or invasions, came in the guise of a friend and ally to harass them as an enemy. The deeds of cruelty, massacre, violence, pillage, arson, imprisoning prelates, burning down monasteries, robbing and killing monks and nuns, and yet other outrages without number which he committed against our people, sparing neither age nor sex, religion nor rank, no one could describe nor fully imagine unless he had seen them with his own eyes.

But from these countless evils we have been set free, by the help of Him Who though He afflicts yet heals and restores, by our most tireless Prince, King and Lord, the Lord Robert. He, that his people and his heritage might be delivered out of the hands of our enemies, met toil and fatigue, hunger and peril, like another Maccabaeus or Joshua and bore them cheerfully. Him, too, divine providence, his right of succession according to our laws and customs which we shall maintain to the death, and the due consent and assent of us all have made our Prince and King. To him, as to the man by whom salvation has been wrought unto our people, we are bound both by law and by his merits that our freedom may be still maintained, and by him, come what may, we mean to stand.

Yet if he should give up what he has begun, and agree to make us or our kingdom subject to the King of England or the English, we should exert ourselves at once to drive him out as our enemy and a subverter of his own rights and ours, and make some other man who was well able to defend us our King; for, as long as but a hundred of us remain alive, never will we on any conditions be brought under English rule. It is in truth not for glory, nor riches, nor honours that we are fighting, but for freedom – for that alone which no honest man gives up but with life itself.

Therefore it is, Reverend Father and Lord, that we beseech your Holiness with our most earnest prayers and suppliant hearts, inasmuch as you will in your sincerity and goodness consider all this, that, since with Him Whose Vice-Regent on earth you are there neither weighing nor distinction of Jew or Greek, Scotsman or Englishman, you will look with the eyes of a father on the troubles and privation brought by the English upon us and upon the Church of God. May it please you to admonish and exhort the King of the English, who ought to be satisfied with what belongs to him since England used once to be enough for seven kings or more, to leave us Scots in peace, who live in this poor little Scotland, beyond which there is no dwelling-place at all, and covet nothing but our own. We are sincerely, willing to do anything for him, having regard to our condition that we can, to win peace for ourselves.

This truly concerns you, Holy Father, since you see the savagery of the heathen raging against the Christians, as the sins of Christians have indeed deserved, and the frontiers of Christendom being pressed inward every day; and how much it will tarnish your Holiness's memory if (which God forbid) the Church suffers eclipse or scandal in any branch of it during your time, you must perceive. Then rouse the Christian princes who for false reasons pretend that they cannot go to help of the Holy Land because of wars they have on hand with their neighbours. The real reason that prevents them is that in making war on their smaller neighbours they find quicker profit and weaker resistance. But how cheerfully our Lord the King and we too would go there if the King of the English would leave us in peace. He from Whom nothing is hidden well knows; and we profess and declare it to you as the Vicar of Christ and to all Christendom.

But if your Holiness puts too much faith in the tales the English tell and will not give sincere belief to all this, nor refrain from favouring them to our prejudice, then the slaughter of bodies, the perdition of souls, and all the other misfortunes that will follow, inflicted by them on us and by us on them, will, we believe, be surely laid by the Most High to your charge.

To conclude, we are and shall ever be, as far as duty calls us, ready to do your will in all things, as obedient sons to you as His Vicar; and to Him as the Supreme King and Judge we commit the maintenance of our cause, casting our cares upon Him and firmly trusting that He will inspire us with courage and bring our enemies to nought.

May the Most High preserve you to his Holy Church in holiness and health and grant you length of days.

Given at the monastery of Arbroath in Scotland on the sixth day of the month of April in the year of grace thirteen hundred and twenty and the fifteenth year of the reign of our King aforesaid.

Endorsed: Letter directed to our Lord the Supreme Pontiff by the community of Scotland...

Luath Press Limited
committed to publishing well written books worth reading

LUATH PRESS takes its name from Robert Burns, whose little collie Luath (*Gael.*, swift or nimble) tripped up Jean Armour at a wedding and gave him the chance to speak to the woman who was to be his wife and the abiding love of his life.

Burns called one of 'The Twa Dogs' Luath after Cuchullin's hunting dog in Ossian's *Fingal*. Luath Press was established in 1981 in the heart of Burns country, and now resides a few steps up the road from Burns' first lodgings on Edinburgh's Royal Mile.

Luath offers you distinctive writing with a hint of unexpected pleasures.

Most bookshops in the UK, the US, Canada, Australia, New Zealand and parts of Europe either carry our books in stock or can order them for you. To order direct from us, please send a £sterling cheque, postal order, international money order or your credit card details (number, address of cardholder and expiry date) to us at the address below. Please add post and packing as follows: UK – £1.00 per delivery address; overseas surface mail – £2.50 per delivery address; overseas airmail – £3.50 for the first book to each delivery address, plus £1.00 for each additional book by airmail to the same address. If your order is a gift, we will happily enclose your card or message at no extra charge.

Luath Press Limited
543/2 Castlehill
The Royal Mile
Edinburgh EH1 2ND
Scotland

Telephone: 0131 225 4326 (24 hours)
email: sales@luath.co.uk
Website: www.luath.co.uk